BULLEID PACIFICS

Nigel Kendall

AMBERLEY

First published 2018

Amberley Publishing
The Hill, Stroud
Gloucestershire, GL5 4EP

www.amberley-books.com

ISBN 978 1 4456 8227 3 (print)
ISBN 978 1 4456 8228 0 (ebook)

British Library Cataloguing in Publication Data.
A catalogue record for this book is available from the British Library.

Origination by Amberley Publishing.
Printed in the UK.

Introduction

Bulleid Pacifics have been a passion in my life for over fifty years. They speeded past just a short distance from my home, carried me to college every day and whisked me to London during my years of weekly commuting. It didn't matter if they were originals or rebuilds – they were Pacifics and they were Bulleids!

It was on 28 September 1960 (only six days after arriving from New Zealand) that I rode my bike from the small Hampshire seaside village of Mudeford out to the Christchurch railway embankment and the Bournemouth to Southampton line. It was only a short wait before a bright plume of steam to the east heralded an approaching train, and within seconds my first Bulleid Pacific, No. 34006 *Bude*, hurried by – brakes groaning for a scheduled stop at Christchurch. I was entranced, and needless to say No. 34006 has always remained my favourite West Country.

From that autumn day onwards I spent much of my life by the local lineside, photographing steam. For seven years, until that dreaded day on 9 July 1967 when SR steam finished, I built a large collection of over 2,500 images; at least 40 per cent were Bulleid Pacifics.

A favourite Bulleid memory is of winter mornings, on my way to work on a local farm. Depending on when I left home, I would be in time to perch on a road bridge and watch the 7.16 a.m. Bournemouth Central to Waterloo charging eastwards through a cutting just south of the farm. But if I was a bit late on a frosty morning, I might still be lucky enough to spot steam just emerging from the oaks to the west, across a meadow. The actual train would be invisible in the cutting, but I would stop and watch the advancing plume as the Merchant Navy or West Country sped eastwards through the landscape. The brilliant white trail of steam would remain in the crisp air as if it had nowhere to go on such a lovely, still morning. Then, after a minute, a long Bulleid 'wail' would echo around the countryside as the train sped through New Milton a mile to the east. I would then gingerly remount my bike and reluctantly pedal my way to work, making sure I didn't come a cropper on the icy track.

One could wax lyrical all day about one's passions, and a love of Bulleid Pacifics is no exception; however, there is another early experience of these fine locomotives and their crews that will always stick with me. It took place on 22 July 1961 at Salisbury, where myself and a friend spent several hours with our cameras. During the day we logged no fewer than seventy-five steam locos, of which thirty-one were Bulleid Pacifics.

What impressed me was the slick routine of engine crews as these mighty beasts arrived and departed the station; and against the grimy GW Castles, Halls and Granges, etc., the procession of shining Merchant Navies and light Pacifics was a delight to see. Many of the firemen would be on the platform, swinging the water crane towards the tender before the Pacific had even stopped! Then, after what seemed a very brief interlude, the crew would jump on board and off they went towards the switchback hills of Devon. Just ten minutes later and another Pacific would draw in and the process would be repeated. It was all exciting stuff to witness.

Another aspect of my addiction to Bulleid Pacifics involved logging their performances during my trips up the main line to Waterloo from my home at New Milton in south-west Hampshire. Often I would get the crew to sign my logbook after a good run, and good runs were frequent, especially in the chaotic final years of electrification.

Southern Region crews really appreciated the power of the Bulleid Pacifics after years of 4-4-0s and 4-6-0s. Yes, the Schools and King Arthur classes were excellent engines, but for pure strength the 'Mercs' and light Pacifics were in a class of their own. They were a fireman's locomotive and raising steam with Mr Bulleid's magnificent boiler gave few concerns.

The exploits of the Bulleid Pacifics have become legendary and several books have been written on the subject. There is one run, however, which stands out for me as a Merchant Navy trip at its best, and it was none other than No. 35028 *Clan Line* which did the honours. Not for this now-preserved engine the joy of a straight, gently profiled main line; with Exmouth Junction's Driver Burridge in charge, and 425 tons behind the tender, *Clan Line* achieved an 83.24 mph average over the 50.5 miles of switchback between Semley and Milepost 151.5, on the Exeter main line. A maximum speed of 104 mph was recorded at Axminster. Waiting passengers on the platform must have been nearly blown away!

Another storming trip, in January 1967, which would have made my adrenalin rush was a run behind rebuilt West Country No. 34098 *Templecombe*, which, with 365 tons behind the tender, averaged 87 mph between Winchfield and Hampton Court Junction – 26.5 miles in 18 min. 16 sec., driven by Nine Elms's Driver Porter. The maximum speed was 95 mph.

Of course, it could be argued that the Bulleid Pacifics were very much the centre of attention for performance recorders during the 1960s, and there are therefore more published logs from which to select. However, this argument could be countered by the fact that Kings, Princesses and A4s, for example, had many more years of operation in which to excel.

But perhaps the greatest test of Bulleid Pacific sheer brute strength is best described here by ex-Nine Elms Fireman Alan Newman, who was Driver Bert Hooker's regular mate:

> I worked the Up 'Royal Wessex' with Driver Bert Hooker over thirty times in my time as his regular Fireman, but one trip stands out from all the others.
>
> One day we had 35011 with 12 coaches (404 tons behind the tender). I was enjoying a good trip, but at Winchester the starting signal remained 'on' for some reason. Apparently a freight train had failed in front of us and Control wanted us to go forward light engine to push the failed train into Wallers Ash loop. We would then return wrong road to retrieve our train. But Bert, being the driver for such occasions, felt that the job would be easier by taking our own train along and using its extra weight to add momentum for starting both trains on the 1/250 gradient. Up for a challenge, we set off and stopped about 10 feet short of the failed train.
>
> The stricken train had a Type 33 diesel with 70 vanfits plus a Brake van. Bert told Alec, the diesel second man, to release the hand brake when the buffers were about 8–10 inches apart. Bert sounded the whistle code to alert the diesel driver and we eased forward and made contact. At this point the momentum started the ensemble up the bank. We were soon up to 15/18 mph with Bert working 35011 at 50 per cent cut off.
>
> With 250 psi of steam and just over 1/2 a glass of water, Bert spurred 35011 into action saying, 'Come on old girl, do it for Gaffer Gilmore,' whose regular engine she was when new. Having cleared the failed train into Wallers Ash Loop, we stopped and waited for Alec to secure the train with the hand brake. Bert then eased our train back and stopped to check that the hand brake was holding the failed train. The Wallers Ash signalman then gave us a green hand signal to back out of the loop and we stopped behind his home signal. Eventually, Waterloo was reached just 30 minutes late. A bit of an anticlimax really!
>
> Bert said it was probably the heaviest train a Merchant Navy ever tackled. He estimated the total weight to be around 1,200 tons, all started on a 1/250 rising gradient without a slip!

Rebuilt or not? This is a question asked many times over the years among Bulleid Pacific enthusiasts. But for what it's worth, my impressions as a performance recorder are that there wasn't much difference between the two versions.

Here, I think ex-Bournemouth Fireman Keith Earl Orchard sums up the opinions of most Footplatemen:

> The 'Spam cans' were astonishing for their designer's innovations, but they were hard work at times, especially the steam reverser, which could be very temperamental.

> The 'recons' [rebuilds] were easier for the Fireman and Driver alike, and when it came to 'squaring up' it was a 'recon' for me every time, but then I am a lazy so and so!

Bob Cartwright, an Eastleigh Fireman, and still a regular Driver today, has this to say about Bulleid Pacifics:

> Like any other steam locomotive the Pacifics could vary between bone shaking, coal-gobbling monsters and smooth riding, very capable engines depending on their state of repair, but the one reliable constant with them was the steaming ability of their boilers. Very rarely did that aspect give any trouble. Having worked on 34064 with its Giesl ejector, it is fair to say that had they lasted a few more years and been subjected to a bit more 'tweaking' they could have ended up as really exceptional locomotives. Without doubt, in both their original and modified form they were impressive looking machines.

Melvyn Cox, ex-Bournemouth Fireman and still working for the railways, has this to say about Bulleid Pacifics:

> To those of us privileged to have had first-hand experience of them in regular service, they were, in either their original or converted form, arguably the ultimate in British steam locomotive design. The boiler was capable of producing steam in abundance, and with a 'belly full' of best Welsh steam coal it would be a simple matter keeping the 'back corners' filled up.
>
> Built with the crew in mind, and with riding qualities likened to a Rolls-Royce, they were truly a Locoman's locomotive.

As a railway photographer my early impressions of Footplatemen were that they were a reserved bunch of chaps – always prepared to give you a nod, but sometimes reluctant to engage in chat while they waited to be off. It was only after several years of line-siding that I realised what a great deal of concentration was needed in the daily work of managing steam and keeping time. Having said this, over the years I got to know quite a few by their first names and when they occasionally saw my photographs they brightened up and became more forthcoming. It also meant a frequent 'chirp' on the whistle as they spotted me on a sunny day by the lineside.

What British Railways steam locomen had in great measure was a very strong camaraderie and sense of humour. It was teamwork at its best and I'm so glad I was around in those days to witness it.

Fireman Bob Cartwright highlights his enthusiasm for the job:

> Saturday 12th June 1965 was the last day of a most memorable week for me. I was in the Holiday relief gang at Eastleigh and my regular mate Des Holley and I had been

booked on Eastleigh's part of 250 loco diagram for the week, Monday to Saturday. Having signed on at 16.46 hours we walked up to the station with travel passes to Southampton. There I made the obligatory can of tea and awaited the arrival of the up Jersey boat train.

On Monday and Tuesday we had 35023 and 35026 respectively, but for the last three days Eastleigh's 34082 *615 Squadron* had turned up on the job. The engine was a favourite of mine. She was the loco on my first boat train from Southampton New Dock to London some months before. She never had a glamorous name, being one of many named after an RAF squadron, but she was a top class loco and, in my experience, equal to many of the Merchant Navies around at that time.

As the train rolled in and stopped right for water I was really pleased to see her on the job yet again. I climbed up on the tender to put the pipe in and Des turned on the supply before talking to the Weymouth Driver about the load and other important matters. The Fireman collected his traps and, leaving the cab, climbed up to take over the pipe, telling me that all was well. I made my way to the cab and there, as was nearly always the case on his job, I found the fire literally rolling out of the door – probably around a ton of red hot fire packed into the box!

The water supply replenished and with clear signals and the right away from the Guard, we departed on our 1 hr 40 min. trip to Waterloo. With the same good loco for the fourth consecutive day my confidence was sky high and it was an outstandingly good trip to round off a week never to be forgotten.

From a photographer's point of view, Bulleid Pacifics were a joy to capture whatever the lighting angles and conditions. I mainly used black and white film for several reasons. Firstly, I was able to develop and print the films in my own little dark room, allowing me some control of the quality. Secondly, producing multiple prints for my enthusiast comrades was easier to do. I used some colour transparency films, but it was expensive and in those days the quality was very variable. It was also a costly exercise to obtain copies.

It's difficult to decide which are my favourite Bulleid Pacific images. My shot of Nine Elms Merchant Navy No. 35017 *Belgian Marine* climbing Hinton Bank has to rate very highly, but a close second is Battle of Britain No. 34052 *Lord Dowding* flying along the Christchurch embankment with an eastbound train. Whatever my favourites, this book is a way of disseminating my Bulleid Pacific photographs to the widest possible audience of enthusiasts, and serves also as a tribute, not only to Oliver Bulleid and his truly unique Pacifics, but also to the Footplatemen whose hard work allowed the spectacle of working steam to enhance the lives of so many railway lovers.

Nigel Kendall
27 February 2018

The Author poses with Merchant Navy No. 35003 *Royal Mail* on Bournemouth Shed on 27 June 1967, just two weeks before the end of SR steam. The loco entered traffic in September 1941 and was rebuilt in August 1959. She was withdrawn in July 1967.

Drifting over a TSR just west of New Milton, West Country No. 34087 *145 Squadron* is heading a Bournemouth to Waterloo service on 2 September 1966. The loco was introduced in December 1948 and was rebuilt in December 1960. Withdrawal was in July 1967.

Moving at speed down Hinton Bank, West Country No. 34108 *Wincanton* is heading a Waterloo to Weymouth express on 6 March 1965. Entering traffic in April 1950, No. 34108 was rebuilt in March 1961 and withdrawn in June 1967.

Clean original Bulleid Pacifics with maroon LMR stock were pretty trains, especially on a sunny Saturday morning. Here, Bournemouth's No. 34102 *Lapford* is in ex-works condition as she pulls into New Milton with the Bournemouth to York inter-regional on 23 August 1962. The loco was introduced in March 1950 and was withdrawn in July 1967, being one of the last original Bulleid Pacifics to survive in BR service.

An uncommon loco on the Bournemouth line, Merchant Navy No. 35009 *Shaw Savill* wakes up sleepy New Milton with a Sunday morning two-hour Waterloo–Bournemouth express in December 1961. *Shaw Savill* entered traffic in June 1942, was rebuilt in March 1957 and withdrawn in September 1964.

Powering past the summit of Hinton Bank on a crisp 5 March 1965, Battle of Britain No. 34089 *602 Squadron* is making light work of a heavy Bournemouth to Waterloo express. This was one of my favourite spots for eastbound trains. The loco was introduced in December 1949 and rebuilt in November 1960. She lasted until the end of SR steam in July 1967.

Looking almost polished in the low late afternoon sun, West Country No. 34009 *Lyme Regis* takes a run at Hinton Bank as she heads east with a two-hour Bournemouth to Waterloo express on 15 August 1961. In the early sixties this loco always seemed to be immaculate. Introduced in September 1949, she was rebuilt in January 1961 and withdrawn in October 1966.

Another West Country climbing Hinton Bank, the 100 milepost marking the end of the incline. This time it's No. 34044 *Woolacombe* with a Weymouth to Waterloo express on 15 November 1961. The loco was introduced to traffic on October 1946 and rebuilt in May 1960. It was withdrawn in May 1967.

On menial station pilot duty at Bournemouth Central on 27 June 1967, Merchant Navy No. 35003 *Royal Mail* looks as if it's resigned to withdrawal in just two weeks' time. On the footplate are Bournemouth's Fireman Bill Stanworth (taking a turn at the regulator) and Driver Frank Hockaday. The loco entered traffic in September 1941 and was rebuilt in August 1959. She was withdrawn in July 1967.

On a hot summer's morning, 3 June 1966, West Country No. 34008 *Padstow* heads east near Stem Lane with a Bournemouth to Waterloo service. Earlier in the sixties, as a Brighton engine, No. 34008 always looked very smart when she headed the Sundays-only Brighton to Bournemouth service through New Milton. Introduced in September 1945 and rebuilt in June 1960, No. 34008 was withdrawn in June 1967.

Shining dully, Merchant Navy No. 35001 *Channel Packet* flies through New Milton with a two-hour Waterloo to Bournemouth express on 17 May 1961. In those days it was uncommon to see an unclean Nine Elms Bulleid Pacific. *Channel Packet* was turned out new in June 1941 and was rebuilt in August 1959. She was withdrawn in November 1964.

West Country No. 34005 *Barnstaple* is looking pretty rough as she arrives at New Milton with a Waterloo-bound service on 16 December 1966. *Barnstaple* entered traffic in July 1945 and was rebuilt in June 1957. She was recorded as withdrawn in October 1966 but was reprieved for pre-Christmas traffic.

Looking very smart following railtour duties, West Country No. 34025 *Whimple* is attracting cross-generation interest at New Milton on 10 June 1967. The loco was in charge of an Eastleigh to Bournemouth local. The Fireman is Dave Tomlin of Eastleigh. The loco entered traffic in March 1946 and was rebuilt in October 1957. Withdrawal was in July 1967.

Merchant Navy No. 35007 *Aberdeen Commonwealth* is struggling on Hinton Bank with a Weymouth to Waterloo express on 17 February 1967. The leaking gland is probably not helping. The Author had an amazing run behind No. 35007 on 3 June 1967 when the loco replaced No. 35030 on the returning 'Dorset Limited' railtour from Waterloo. The loco entered traffic in June 1942 and was rebuilt in May 1958. It was withdrawn in July 1967.

Minus nameplates, but steam tight and going well, Eastleigh's Battle of Britain Pacific No. 34087 *145 Squadron* erupts through New Milton with a Weymouth to Waterloo express on 19 August 1966. A good performer right until the end of SR steam in July 1967, No. 34087 was introduced to traffic in December 1948 and rebuilt in December 1960.

Bournemouth's West Country Pacific No. 34005 *Barnstaple* is in superb condition as she flies through New Milton with a Weymouth to Waterloo express on 19 August 1966. *Barnstaple* was the first West Country to be rebuilt, in June 1957, having entered traffic in July 1945. She also took part in the 1948 locomotive exchanges on St Pancras to Manchester Central services. Sadly, No. 34005 was withdrawn just two months after this photograph was taken.

Bournemouth's Driver Fred Davies and Fireman Chris Doel look for a green flag while crewing Battle of Britain No. 34077 *603 Squadron* on a Bournemouth to Eastleigh local at New Milton on 10 May 1966. The loco was introduced to traffic in July 1948 and was rebuilt in July 1960. She lasted until March 1967 before being withdrawn.

Photographed from one of my favourite locations, on the roof of a gangers hut west of Stem Lane, Merchant Navy No. 35010 *Blue Star* is hurrying west with a Waterloo to Weymouth express on 29 May 1966. Introduced in July 1942, No. 35010 was rebuilt in January 1957 and withdrawn in September 1966.

Battle of Britain No. 34082 *615 Squadron* looks in ex-works condition under that cloak of steam. A Nine Elms loco, she is seen pulling out of New Milton with a westbound Waterloo to Bournemouth West service on 16 March 1961. The loco was introduced in September 1948 and rebuilt in April 1960. She was withdrawn in April 1966.

Eastleigh's Battle of Britain No. 34084 *253 Squadron* is a fine sight as she accelerates through Boscombe with a Bournemouth Central to Waterloo express on 8 April 1965, my twentieth birthday. Initially allocated to Stewarts Lane in November 1948, No. 34084 was withdrawn in October 1965.

The original West Country Pacific, No. 34001 *Exeter*, looks a fine sight at New Milton on 14 January 1962 while heading a Waterloo to Bournemouth West service. My only trip behind No. 34001 was in May 1967, when pre-electrification engineering resulted in Southampton to Waterloo services being diverted via Fareham, Havant and Guildford, rejoining the Waterloo main line at Woking. A long drawn-out journey but full of interest. *Exeter* was introduced into traffic in June 1945 and rebuilt in November 1957. She was withdrawn in July 1967.

A long-serving Bournemouth loco, West Country No. 34041 *Wilton* draws out of New Milton with the York to Bournemouth West inter-regional service on 21 May 1961. *Wilton* was a stalwart of the S&D route to Bath for several years. She was introduced to traffic in October 1946 and eventually withdrawn in January 1966.

Minus nameplates, West Country Pacific No. 34048 *Crediton* creates some drama as it pulls out of New Milton with a Down Waterloo to Bournemouth service on 13 February 1965. Entering traffic in November 1948, No. 34048 was rebuilt in March 1959 and withdrawn in March 1966.

A special working speeds up through New Milton behind Battle of Britain Pacific No. 34060 *25 Squadron* on 30 July 1965. I had an amazing run from Southampton to Waterloo behind this engine on 21 May 1967. Five separate maxima of over 80 mph were obtained between Basingstoke and New Malden. The crew were Fireman Old and Driver Reg Ward of Bournemouth Shed. The loco entered traffic in April 1947 and was rebuilt in November 1960. She was withdrawn in July 1967.

Carefully negotiating a temporary speed restriction, West Country No. 34093 *Saunton* is heading a Weymouth to Waterloo express just west of New Milton. The Author had an excellent run out of Waterloo behind No. 34093 in 1967, arriving in Southampton eight minutes early despite two speed restrictions and a long signal check. *Saunton* was rolled out in October 1949 and rebuilt in May 1960. Her withdrawal was in July 1967.

Hinton Bank was the last opportunity for speed before reaching Bournemouth Central, so locomotives were regularly spurred on to pick up time. Here, Eastleigh's West Country No. 34098 *Templecombe* speeds down the gradient with a Waterloo to Weymouth express on 6 March 1965. The loco was introduced in December 1949 and rebuilt in February 1961. She was withdrawn from service in June 1967.

Eastleigh's West Country No. 34095 *Brentor* stands at New Milton with a Waterloo to Bournemouth service on 12 June 1965. The loco was out-shopped from Eastleigh Works in October 1949 and rebuilt in January 1961. She lasted until the end of SR steam in July 1967.

With Nine Elms Fireman Alan Newman just visible, the early morning 'Royal Wessex' accelerates away from Bournemouth Central with Merchant Navy No. 35011 *General Steam Navigation* in charge on 14 April 1963. On 31 August 1963 the Author recorded a superb run behind this loco, averaging 76.2 mph over the 31.2 miles between Berrylands and Hook on the Waterloo to Southampton main line. She was introduced to traffic in December 1944, rebuilt in August 1957 and withdrawn in February 1966.

An eastbound parcels train passes New Milton's recently lifted goods yard behind West Country No. 34100 *Appledore* on 9 June 1967. Evidence of No. 34100's past service as a 'Golden Arrow' engine can be seen by the arrow fixing studs on the smoke deflector. The loco was introduced in December 1949 and rebuilt in September 1960. She was withdrawn from traffic in July 1967.

A nice portrait of West Country No. 34105 *Swanage* as she pulls out of New Milton with a westbound inter-regional service on 20 June 1961. *Swanage* was a Bournemouth loco from new until it was reallocated to Eastleigh in September 1964. Thankfully she is now under preservation on the Mid-Hants Railway. Having been introduced to traffic in February 1950, No. 34105 was eventually withdrawn in October 1964.

Battle of Britain No. 34087 *145 Squadron* at the head of a Waterloo to Bournemouth service at New Milton on 17 April 1967. The crew are Eastleigh's Driver Ben George and Fireman Brian Harding. The loco was introduced to traffic in December 1948, rebuilt in December 1960 and withdrawn in July 1967.

Merchant Navy No. 35013 *Blue Funnel* is looking smart as it draws a Waterloo to Bournemouth service out of New Milton on 2 February 1967. Introduced to traffic in February 1945, *Blue Funnel* was rebuilt in May 1956 and withdrawn at the end of SR steam in July 1967.

Heading a van train through New Milton on 1 July 1967, Bournemouth's West Country No. 34025 *Whimple* is in excellent external condition following railtour duty. The loco was introduced to traffic in March 1946, rebuilt in October 1957 and withdrawn in July 1967. Note the recently lifted goods yard.

Flying through New Milton on a dull 20 April 1967, Merchant Navy No. 35007 *Aberdeen Commonwealth* is in charge of a late-running Waterloo to Weymouth express. The loco was introduced to traffic in June 1942 and was rebuilt in May 1948. She lasted until the end of SR steam in July 1967.

Eastleigh's West Country No. 34042 *Dorchester* heads east on the Christchurch embankment with a Bournemouth to Waterloo service on 21 May 1965. *Dorchester* was introduced to traffic in October 1946 and was rebuilt in January 1959. She was withdrawn in October 1965.

Heading an Up Weymouth to Waterloo express, Merchant Navy No. 35003 *Royal Mail* is going well past New Milton goods yard on 13 May 1966. On 15 October 1965 the Author recorded an average of 78 mph between Surbiton and Woking behind No. 35003 working the 17.30 ex-Waterloo. Having been introduced to traffic in September 1941, No. 35003 was rebuilt in August 1959 and withdrawn in July 1967.

Eastleigh's West Country No. 34018 *Axminster* passes Walkford with a Waterloo to Weymouth express on 9 May 1966. *Axminster* was new out of Works in December 1945, rebuilt in September 1958 and withdrawn in July 1967.

A powerful image of Nine Elms Merchant Navy No. 35014 *Nederland Line* hurrying through New Milton on the Waterloo-bound 'Royal Wessex' on 14 May 1964. The loco was new to traffic in February 1945 and rebuilt in July 1956. She was withdrawn in March 1967.

Picked out by a winter sun, Bournemouth's West Country No. 34028 *Eddystone* is steam tight and going well with a Bournemouth to Waterloo express on 15 November 1961. The Author travelled behind this loco over the S&D from Poole to Bath on the 'Pines Express' in August 1962. She was introduced to traffic in May 1946, rebuilt in August 1958 and withdrawn in May 1964.

A superbly turned-out Brighton loco, West Country No. 34027 *Taw Valley* runs through New Milton with the Sundays-only Brighton to Bournemouth West excursion on 21 July 1961. Now a preserved loco, No. 34027 was introduced in April 1946 and rebuilt in November 1957. She was withdrawn in August 1964.

A Bournemouth stalwart, West Country No. 34103 *Calstock* hurries through Eastleigh with a Bournemouth-bound inter-regional service from Sheffield on 24 August 1962. *Calstock* was also a frequent engine on the Somerset & Dorset to Bath. She was introduced to traffic in February 1950 and withdrawn from service in September 1965.

Fireman Barry Sullivan looks dejected following the arrival at Waterloo of the 'Dorset Limited' railtour from Bournemouth Central on 3 June 1967. The train was headed by Merchant Navy No. 35030 *Elder-Dempster Line*. The special was scheduled to reach London in 116 minutes, breaking the existing record. It is alleged that an on-board inspector tapped Driver Sanson on the shoulder as we approached 90 mph and said, 'That's enough Bill,' which had the effect of causing a three minute late arrival. Having been introduced in April 1949, No. 35030 was rebuilt in April 1958 and withdrawn in July 1967.

West Country No. 34043 *Combe Martin* is running well just west of New Milton with an eastbound express for Waterloo on 22 April 1962. Having been a Bournemouth loco since 1952, No. 34043 was introduced in October 1946 and withdrawn in June 1963.

Eastleigh's Battle of Britain No. 34090 *Sir Eustace Missenden, Southern Railway* makes a smoky start from New Milton with a Waterloo to Bournemouth service on 4 September 1965. This loco was originally intended to be the last Bulleid light Pacific to be built and was therefore named after the last General Manager of the Southern Railway. In the event, a further twenty engines were built. Introduced in February 1949, No. 34090 was rebuilt in August 1960 and withdrawn in July 1967.

On 31 December 1964 a Merchant Navy pulls into Brockenhurst while West Country No. 34017 *Ilfracombe* pauses in the opposite platform with a Waterloo to Bournemouth service. Introduced in December 1945, No. 34017 was rebuilt in November 1957 and withdrawn from service in October 1966.

In the appalling winter of 1962/63, Eastleigh's West Country No. 34038 *Lynton* struggles eastward near Walkford with a service for Waterloo. Despite the conditions, Bulleid Pacifics did a fine job of keeping traffic moving on the Bournemouth and Weymouth main line. *Lynton* was photographed on 14 January 1963. Introduced to traffic in September 1946, No. 34038 was eventually withdrawn in June 1966.

It's a bitterly cold 7 March 1964 and Merchant Navy No. 35028 *Clan Line* is making good progress on Hinton Bank with the 'Bournemouth Belle' Pullman to Waterloo. In preservation No. 35028 is still a superb performer on regular railtours in the south of England. *Clan Line* was introduced to traffic in December 1948 and rebuilt in October 1959. The loco worked until the end of SR steam in July 1967, before preservation.

The 'Pines Express' accelerates through Boscombe headed by West Country No. 34040 *Crewkerne* on 8 April 1965. Having spent periods shedded at Bath Green Park, No. 34040 would have been a regular performer on the 'Pines Express' over its original Somerset & Dorset routing. The loco was introduced in September 1946, rebuilt in October 1960 and withdrawn in July 1967.

Speeding west near Sway, Nine Elms Battle of Britain No. 34073 *249 Squadron* heads a two-hour Waterloo to Bournemouth Central express on 10 September 1962. This loco was originally shedded at Ramsgate before spending twelve years at Dover, then moving to the South Western Division in 1961. Introduced to traffic in May 1948, No. 34073 was eventually withdrawn in June 1964.

A special train, the 'Dorset Limited' enters Bournemouth Central behind Merchant Navy No. 35030 *Elder-Dempster Line* on 2 June 1967. It was organised to attempt a non-stop record run of 116 minutes between Bournemouth Central and Waterloo. In the event, No. 35030 arrived at Waterloo in 119 minutes, although the net time was just 106 minutes. The loco was introduced in April 1949 and rebuilt in April 1958. She was withdrawn in July 1967.

A winter's evening at New Milton and Merchant Navy No. 35013 *Blue Funnel*, looking smart after railtour duty, restarts a Waterloo to Weymouth service on 2 February 1967. My only trip on the 'Bournemouth Belle' was behind this loco, in September 1964. She was introduced to traffic in February 1945 and rebuilt in May 1956. Withdrawal was in July 1967.

West Country No. 34102 *Lapford* hurries down through New Milton with an inter-regional service from Manchester on 14 June 1964. I had an excellent run from Waterloo to Southampton behind No. 34102 with a heavy train in August 1965. The loco was introduced in March 1950 and withdrawn in July 1967. *Lapford* was the last unmodified Bulleid Pacific to see action before the end of SR steam.

It was uncommon to see unmodified Bulleid Pacifics on the 'Bournemouth Belle' during the sixties. Here, Eastleigh's West Country No. 34033 *Chard* is in good nick as she races westward down Hinton Bank on 5 March 1965. *Chard* was introduced in June 1946 and withdrawn in December 1965.

With some late snow still lying, Bournemouth's West Country No. 34046 *Braunton* hurries down Hinton Bank with a Waterloo to Weymouth express on 5 March 1965. A regular on the Somerset & Dorset, No. 34046 was introduced in November 1946, rebuilt February 1959 and withdrawn in October 1965.

Shorn of nameplates, Eastleigh's Battle of Britain No. 34088 *213 Squadron* is turned on Bournemouth's turntable on 8 March 1965. She was introduced in December 1948, rebuilt in April 1960 and withdrawn in March 1967.

On 26 March 1965, with just two months to go before withdrawal, West Country No. 34039 *Boscastle* climbs Hinton Bank with a Weymouth to Waterloo express. The loco was introduced in September 1946, rebuilt in January 1959 and withdrawn in May 1965. Note the superb lineside maintenance.

Crossing cautiously over to the Down line at New Milton during engineering work, Bournemouth's West Country No. 34012 *Launceston* is heading an eastbound express for Waterloo on 9 May 1966. Although in a sorry external state, the loco appears to be in good running order. She was introduced in October 1945, rebuilt in January 1958 and withdrawn in December 1966.

Merchant Navy No. 35008 *Orient Line* blasts through New Milton with the London-bound 'Channel Islands Boat Express' from Weymouth Pier on 1 July 1967. The Author had five runs to London Waterloo behind this loco during the sixties and each one involved fine running with both Nine Elms and Bournemouth crews. It was introduced in June 1942 and was rebuilt in May 1957. The loco lasted until the end of SR steam in July 1967.

In an appalling external condition, West Country No. 34036 *Westward Ho* drifts through New Milton with a westbound express on 18 April 1967. I had three trips behind this loco between Waterloo and Southampton. Each of them would have been early arrivals at Central station had it not been for last-minute signal checks. She was introduced in July 1946, rebuilt in August 1960 and withdrawn in July 1967.

An early evening shot of Eastleigh's West Country No. 34017 *Ilfracombe* waiting at New Milton with a local from Eastleigh to Bournemouth on 27 December 1964. *Ilfracombe* was introduced in December 1945, rebuilt in November 1957 and withdrawn in October 1966.

Accelerating between Lymington Junction and Sway, West Country No. 34001 *Exeter* is in charge of a Waterloo to Weymouth service on 25 August 1963. I have fond memories of No. 34001 taking me from Southampton to Waterloo via Fareham, Havant, Guildford and Woking in May 1967 due to electrification work. It was slow, but interesting. *Exeter* was introduced in June 1945 and rebuilt in November 1957. She was withdrawn in July 1967.

Nine Elms West Country No. 34002 *Salisbury* drifts into New Milton with a Bournemouth to Waterloo service on 4 September 1965. A cheer would always go up from trainspotters on Salisbury station when No. 34002 rolled in! The loco was introduced in June 1945 and she was withdrawn in April 1967.

A vicar, grandmother, and businessman take little interest in Bournemouth's West Country No. 34004 *Yeovil* at Bournemouth Central on 29 June 1967. In April 1967 the Author had a splendid run behind this loco when it made up eight minutes of lost time between Southampton and Waterloo due to engineering work. She was introduced in June 1945, rebuilt in February 1958 and withdrawn in October 1966.

One of my favourite Merchant Navy photographs, taken during the severe winter of 1962/63. No. 35005 *Canadian Pacific* powers through New Milton with a two-hour Bournemouth Central to Waterloo express on 21 January 1963. This loco also thrilled me when, in May 1964, it accelerated from a stop at Winchester to 75 mph at Roundwood, achieving over 2,200 drawbar horsepower in the process. The loco was introduced in January 1942 and was rebuilt in May 1959. It was withdrawn for preservation in October 1965.

West of Stem Lane, my favourite Bulleid light Pacific, West Country No. 34006 *Bude*, hurries westward with a Waterloo to Bournemouth Central two-hour express. As usual in the early sixties, Nine Elms cleaners had been at work. *Bude* was introduced in August 1945 and eventually withdrawn in March 1967.

Having completed a superb run down from Waterloo, West Country No. 34021 *Dartmoor* takes water at Southampton Central on 18 May 1967. A friend who continued on the train to Bournemouth recorded 91 mph down Hinton Bank. *Dartmoor* was introduced in January 1946, rebuilt in December 1957 and withdrawn from service in July 1967.

Merchant Navy No. 35015 *Rotterdam Lloyd* erupts through New Milton with the Waterloo-bound 'Channel Islands Boat Express' on 20 November 1961. I never saw this Nine Elms loco in an unclean condition. It was introduced in March 1945, rebuilt in June 1958 and withdrawn in February 1964.

In the failing evening light, a Weymouth to Waterloo express forges past the New Milton goods yard on 2 February 1967 headed by Merchant Navy No. 35014 *Nederland Line*. Although in a poor external condition, the loco is steam tight and well up to the job. She was introduced in February 1945 and rebuilt in July 1956. She was withdrawn in March 1967.

On a snowy 27 December 1964, Battle of Britain No. 34052 *Lord Dowding* charges through New Milton with a Weymouth to Waterloo express. This loco was a Salisbury engine from June 1951 and was usually very clean. On this occasion, maybe the hard winter prevented cleaners doing their job. The loco was introduced in December 1946 and rebuilt in September 1958. She was withdrawn in July 1967 and subsequently restored.

Merchant Navy No. 35007 *Aberdeen Commonwealth* bursts under the New Milton road bridge and speeds eastward with a Weymouth to Waterloo express on 12 May 1967. I had an amazing run behind No. 35007 from Waterloo to Bournemouth on the returning 'Dorset Limited' special in June 1967. Four individual 80 mph-plus maxima were achieved with Driver Bill Sanson and Fireman Barry Sullivan on the footplate. *Aberdeen Commonwealth* was introduced in June 1942, rebuilt in May 1958 and withdrawn in July 1967 at the end of SR steam.

A rare photograph of the 'Pines Express' headboard being carried over the new routing after the S&D closure. Bournemouth's West Country No. 34102 *Lapford* does the honours as the train heads east between Ashley and Sway on 10 September 1962. *Lapford* was introduced in March 1950 and was withdrawn in July 1967.

New Milton Signalman Len Simpson delivers the tablet to Bournemouth Fireman Chris Doel during single line working on 25 March 1966. The engine is West Country No. 34023 *Blackmore Vale* at the head of a Bournemouth to Waterloo service. She was introduced in February 1946 and withdrawn in July 1967.

Very clean but without nameplates, West Country No. 34025 *Whimple* drifts through New Milton with a westbound van train on 1 July 1967. The loco had been used on railtour duty during April of that year and obviously the buffing-up had been maintained. *Whimple* was introduced in March 1946, rebuilt in October 1957 and withdrawn at the end of SR steam in July 1967.

The driver of Battle of Britain No. 34087 *145 Squadron* appears mesmerised by the track beneath him as his steed lifts a Waterloo to Bournemouth service out of New Milton on 2 September 1966. Introduced in December 1948, No. 34087 was rebuilt in December 1960 and withdrawn in July 1967.

Adhering to a speed restriction at New Milton, West Country No. 34004 *Yeovil* is heading a westbound railtour on 10 June 1967. In April 1967 I had an excellent run behind No. 34004, turning an eight minute late start from Winchester into a one minute early arrival at Waterloo. The loco was introduced in June 1945, rebuilt in February 1958 and withdrawn in July 1967.

Signalman Len Simpson takes the token from the driver of Eastleigh's West Country No. 34037 *Clovelly* during single line working at New Milton on 25 March 1966. The service is a Waterloo to Weymouth express. Introduced in August 1946, No. 34037 was rebuilt in March 1958 and withdrawn in July 1967.

The sun sets over Eastleigh as West Country No. 34047 *Callington* forges east with a Waterloo-bound express on a freezing 31 December 1964. *Callington* was introduced to traffic in November 1946, rebuilt in November 1958 and withdrawn in June 1967.

Brighton's Battle of Britain No. 34057 *Biggin Hill* still sports an unmodified tender as she heads west of New Milton with the Sundays-only Brighton to Bournemouth excursion. This loco, among others, was allocated to the Eastern Region's Stratford shed from May 1951 to May 1952 while faults on the Britannia Pacifics were rectified. *Biggin Hill* was introduced to traffic in March 1947 and was withdrawn in May 1967.

The 'Channel Islands Boat Express' from Weymouth Quay hurries eastwards through New Milton headed by Battle of Britain No. 34060 *25 Squadron* on 26 June 1967. In May 1967 I recorded an excellent run behind this loco driven by Driver Reg Ward and Fireman Old of Bournemouth Shed. The loco achieved five separate 80 mph maxima between Winchester and Waterloo, turning a twenty-minute deficit at Worting Junction into just 5 minutes' lateness at Waterloo. The loco was introduced to traffic in April 1947 and rebuilt in November 1960. She was withdrawn in July 1967.

With holidaymakers waiting patiently, Battle of Britain No. 34071 *601 Squadron* pulls into New Milton with an inter-regional service to York on 14 August 1966. The loco has its nameplate missing but still carries the squadron shield. This loco was introduced into traffic in April 1948 – the first Bulleid light Pacific to be built under BR. It was rebuilt in May 1960 and withdrawn in April 1967.

With a remarkably clean exhaust, Weymouth's Merchant Navy No. 35026 *Lamport & Holt Line* is about to pass through Hinton Admiral station with a Waterloo to Weymouth express on 14 May 1965. Introduced to traffic in December 1948, No. 35026 was rebuilt in January 1957 and withdrawn in March 1967.

Bournemouth Fireman Ronald Whittaker takes a breather at New Milton before restarting with a Bournemouth to Waterloo service on 3 June 1966. The loco is Eastleigh-based Battle of Britain No. 34071 *601 Squadron*. This loco was introduced into traffic in April 1948. It was rebuilt in May 1960 and withdrawn in April 1967.

With its nameplate still intact, West Country No. 34047 *Callington* pulls into New Milton with a Bournemouth to Waterloo train on 3 February 1967. The engine travelled widely in its career, having been shedded at Exmouth Junction, Salisbury, Brighton, Nine Elms and finally Bournemouth. It was introduced to traffic in November 1946, rebuilt in November 1958 and withdrawn in June 1967.

Unclean but steam tight, Merchant Navy No. 35023 *Holland-Afrika Line* hurries through New Milton with a Weymouth to Waterloo express on 31 March 1967. Note the coal bunkers full of semaphore signal remnants following resignalling in the area. One of the last Merchant Navies to run, No. 35023 was introduced in November 1948, rebuilt in February 1957 and withdrawn in July 1967.

An ex-Stewarts Lane 'Golden Arrow' engine, now shedded at Nine Elms, West Country No. 34101 *Hartland* is at speed down Hinton Bank with a Waterloo to Weymouth express on 18 June 1965. The loco was introduced to traffic in February 1950 and rebuilt in September 1960. She was withdrawn in July 1966.

While BR Standard Class 4 No. 76033 simmers in New Milton's goods yard, Salisbury's super-clean West Country No. 34032 *Camelford* erupts through the station with a Weymouth-bound express on 17 August 1965. Although Salisbury's No. 34052 *Lord Dowding* was quite frequent locally, No. 34032 didn't appear so often. She was introduced to traffic in June 1946 and eventually withdrawn in October 1966.

Eastleigh's Battle of Britain No. 34058 *Sir Frederick Pile* waits at New Milton with a Bournemouth to Eastleigh local on 15 August 1964. Three-coach locals were light work for a Pacific and one wonders why Eastleigh sometimes didn't have smaller engines to do the job. The loco was introduced to traffic in April 1947 and rebuilt in November 1960. It was withdrawn in October 1964.

Still sporting an old Dover shedplate, 74C, Battle of Britain No. 34082 *615 Squadron* pulls into New Milton with a Bournemouth to Waterloo service on 16 June 1961. The loco had been reallocated to Nine Elms a month before. She was introduced to traffic in September 1948, rebuilt in April 1960 and withdrawn in April 1966.

Wearing a very unusual headcode, Bournemouth's West Country No. 34043 *Combe Martin* is terminating its train at New Milton after traversing the Salisbury, Fordingbridge, West Moors, Broadstone and Poole line with an inter-regional service from the West Midlands. The date was 2 May 1962. *Combe Martin*, a regular S&D engine, was introduced to traffic in October 1946 and eventually withdrawn in June 1963.

In a hurry with a Waterloo to Weymouth express, Eastleigh's West Country No. 34017 *Ilfracombe* flies through Hinton Admiral on 21 May 1965. The loco was introduced in December 1945, rebuilt in November 1957 and withdrawn in October 1966.

My favourite Merchant Navy, No. 35008 *Orient Line*, rockets past the New Milton goods yard with the eastbound 'Bournemouth Belle' on 13 May 1966. I was travelling behind No. 35008 when it broke the record for the fastest run between Southampton and Waterloo without exceeding the 85 mph speed limit. Despite two engineering speed restrictions and two signal checks, it covered the 79.25 mile trip in just 76 mins 23 secs. Driver McGlaggon and Fireman Alan Newman from Nine Elms were on the footplate. *Orient Line* was introduced to traffic in June 1942, rebuilt in May 1957 and withdrawn in July 1967.

The 'Bournemouth Belle' headed by Eastleigh's West Country No. 34001 *Exeter* climbs Hinton Bank on 10 June 1966. *Exeter* was introduced in June 1945 and rebuilt in November 1957. She was withdrawn in July 1967.

Driver Alf Boston of Bournemouth waits for the guard's green flag at New Milton on 27 December 1964. Battle of Britain No. 34085 *501 Squadron* was a Bournemouth 'good 'un' during the 1960s. It was frequently seen hauling the 'Pines Express' following re-routing in 1963. The loco was introduced in November 1948 and rebuilt in June 1960. It was withdrawn in September 1965.

Sadly, New Milton's goods yard has recently been torn up as West Country No. 34093 *Saunton* adheres to a speed restriction through the station on 10 June 1967. I had a sparkling run from Waterloo to Southampton in May 1967 when No. 34093 arrived over eight minutes early. The loco was introduced to traffic in October 1949, rebuilt in May 1960 and withdrawn in July 1967.

Merchant Navy No. 35026 *Lamport & Holt Line* accelerates away from New Milton with a Bournemouth to Waterloo service on 17 August 1965. Strangely, it has the car registration plate 'ORU 171' on its buffer beam. The loco was introduced to traffic in December 1948, rebuilt in January 1957 and withdrawn in March 1967.

A summer Saturday relief hurries through New Milton headed by Nine Elms West Country No. 34094 *Mortehoe* on 21 June 1962. With Bournemouth, No. 34094 served on only two sheds in its whole career. The loco was introduced to traffic in October 1949 and was withdrawn in August 1964.

Bournemouth's Merchant Navy No. 35011 *General Steam Navigation* draws slowly out of New Milton with a Waterloo to Bournemouth service on 19 June 1965. I had an excellent run behind this loco on 'The Royal Wessex' between Waterloo and Southampton in April 1963. It arrived at Winchester four minutes early and at Southampton Central two minutes early. Its average speed for the 31.18 miles between Berrylands and Hook was 76.2 mph. *General Steam Navigation* was introduced to traffic in December 1944, rebuilt in July 1959 and withdrawn in February 1966.

On one of those bright winter's days we used to enjoy in the sixties, Salisbury's West Country No. 34012 *Launceston* speeds down Hinton Bank with a Waterloo to Weymouth express on 6 March 1965. The loco was introduced to traffic in October 1945, rebuilt in January 1958 and withdrawn in December 1966.

Weymouth's Merchant Navy No. 35022 *Holland America Line* is looking very clean as she accelerates out of Pokesdown with a Bournemouth to Waterloo service on 8 March 1965. This engine was the last to head the 'Atlantic Coast Express' on an eighty-minute schedule from Waterloo to Salisbury. Introduced in October 1948, No. 35022 was rebuilt in June 1956 and withdrawn in May 1966.

Waiting at Hinton Admiral with a Bournemouth to Eastleigh local, Eastleigh's Battle of Britain No. 34050 *Royal Observer Corps* looks very smart in the setting sun on 26 March 1965. The loco was introduced to traffic in December 1946, rebuilt in August 1958 and withdrawn in August 1965.

A Bournemouth West to Waterloo service arrives at New Milton headed by West Country No. 34105 *Swanage* on 22 July 1962. A Bournemouth Shed loco for its entire working life, No. 34105 has lasted into preservation and I have had the pleasure of riding on its footplate several times. Introduced in February 1950, the loco was withdrawn from traffic in October 1964.

The last Merchant Navy to be built, No. 35030 *Elder-Dempster Lines* charges through Hinton Admiral with the westbound 'Bournemouth Belle' on 27 March 1965. This loco was introduced to traffic in April 1949, rebuilt in April 1948 and withdrawn in July 1967.

My 'natural habitat' during the sixties. I saw most of the Bulleid Pacifics on through traffic at New Milton and occasionally on early morning shunting duties in the yard – usually ex-works locos running-in. Here, West Country No. 34034 *Honiton* waits in the Down platform with a Waterloo to Bournemouth West service on 2 May 1962. *Honiton* was introduced to traffic in July 1946 and was rebuilt in August 1960. She was withdrawn at the end of steam in July 1967.

A lovely warm summer's day at Bournemouth Central and Battle of Britain No. 34066 *Spitfire* slowly draws out with a Bournemouth to Waterloo service on 12 September 1964. At the time of this photograph the locomotive had only just been transferred from Exmouth Junction to Salisbury. Introduced to traffic in September 1947, No. 34066 lasted until September 1966 before withdrawal.

Due to its filthy condition, there are no reflections on Eastleigh's Battle of Britain No. 34084 *253 Squadron* as it accelerates into the setting sun after a stop at Sway on 30 December 1964. It was introduced in November 1948 and withdrawn in October 1965.

With only two months to go before withdrawal, and going well with a Weymouth to Waterloo express, Eastleigh's West Country No. 34103 *Calstock* erupts through New Milton on 16 July 1965. *Calstock* was introduced in February 1950 and withdrawn on September 1965.

With a local gardener showing more interest in his leeks, Bournemouth's Merchant Navy No. 35011 *General Steam Navigation* powers past with a Weymouth to Waterloo express on 13 July 1964. The loco was introduced in December 1944, rebuilt in July 1959 and withdrawn in February 1966.

In charge of the 'Bournemouth Belle,' Nine Elms Driver Jim Robinson is keen to be off with Merchant Navy No. 35014 *Nederland Line*, at Bournemouth Central on 1 October 1965. Ending its days as a Weymouth engine, No. 35014 was introduced in February 1945, rebuilt in July 1956 and withdrawn in March 1967.

With a Weymouth crew at the helm, the 'Channel Islands Boat Express' from Weymouth Quay passes Talbot Heath, Bournemouth, headed by West Country No. 34097 *Holsworthy* on 1 October 1965. The loco was introduced in November 1949, rebuilt in February 1961 and withdrawn in April 1966.

In pouring rain, Eastleigh's West Country No. 34034 *Honiton* passes Talbot Heath, near Bournemouth, with an eastbound train on 1 October 1965. *Honiton* was introduced to traffic in July 1946, rebuilt in August 1960 and withdrawn in July 1967.

In a train of three condemned locos, West Country No. 34045 *Ottery St Mary* is destined for Woodham Bros in South Wales while Battle of Britain No. 34051 *Winston Churchill* takes water at Salisbury on 23 February 1965. I followed the train up the Wylye Valley to Westbury where No. 34051 came off. *Ottery St Mary* was introduced to traffic in October 1946, rebuilt in October 1958 and withdrawn in June 1964.

Nine Elms Merchant Navy No. 35020 *Bibby Line* is in fine condition as she pushes the recently arrived 'Bournemouth Belle' out of Bournemouth West and through the washing plant on 21 July 1962. This loco was introduced in June 1945, rebuilt in April 1956 and withdrawn in February 1965.

Hauling a short Sundays-only excursion from Brighton to Bournemouth, Battle of Britain No. 34057 *Biggin Hill* has an easy ride down Hinton Bank on 26 November 1963. The loco was introduced in March 1947 and withdrawn from traffic in May 1967.

Drifting into New Milton, Bournemouth's long-term resident Merchant Navy No. 35027 *Port Line* is heading a Bournemouth to Waterloo service on 30 July 1965. *Port Line* was introduced in December 1948, rebuilt in May 1957 and withdrawn into preservation in September 1966.

Passing through Pokesdown with the 'Channel Islands Boat Express', Weymouth Merchant Navy No. 35003 *Royal Mail* is in good condition, but without nameplates, on 12 May 1967. This loco was introduced to traffic in September 1941, rebuilt in August 1959 and withdrawn at the end of SR steam in July 1967.

In the late afternoon sun, West Country No. 34013 *Okehampton* passes BR4 2-6-0 No. 76057 while heading a Bournemouth to Waterloo service into New Milton on 2 September 1966. *Okehampton* was introduced to traffic in October 1945 and rebuilt in October 1957. She was withdrawn in July 1967.

Despite its poor state and without nameplates, West Country Pacific No. 34019 *Bideford* appears to be strong enough as it speeds west near New Milton with a Waterloo to Bournemouth express on 2 December 1966. Entering traffic in December 1945, No. 34019 was withdrawn in March 1967.

Steam managed to struggle on over the Bournemouth main line during the dreadful winter of 1962/63, but it must have been very difficult for crews and depot maintenance men. Here, Merchant Navy No. 35005 *Canadian Pacific* forges up Hinton Bank with a Weymouth to Waterloo express on 21 January 1963. Now preserved, No. 35005 entered traffic in January 1942 and was rebuilt in May 1959. It was withdrawn in October 1965.

During the last days of steam at Bournemouth Central, West Country No. 34021 *Dartmoor* draws into the station with an Up train behind a BR4 2-6-0, while No. 34024 *Tamar Valley* awaits its next duty on the shed. Photographed on 29 June 1967, *Dartmoor* entered traffic on January 1946, was rebuilt in December 1957 and was withdrawn in July 1967.

In typical Salisbury condition, the shed's Battle of Britain No. 34056 *Croydon* pulls out of New Milton with a Waterloo-bound service on 19 August 1966. The loco entered traffic in February 1947, was rebuilt in December 1960 and was withdrawn in May 1967.

The woods echo to the roar of a toiling Merchant Navy climbing Hinton Bank with a two-hour Bournemouth to Waterloo express on 25 September 1964. The engine is Weymouth's No. 35019 *French Line CGT*. She was introduced to traffic in June 1945, rebuilt in May 1959 and withdrawn in September 1965.

A warm summer's day and Weymouth's Merchant Navy No. 35017 *Belgian Marine* hurries through New Milton hauling the eastbound 'Channel Islands Boat Express' on 6 August 1964. *Belgian Marine* entered traffic in April 1945 and was rebuilt in March 1957. She was withdrawn in July 1966.

Filthy and without nameplates, West Country No. 34012 *Launceston* hurries through New Milton with the 'Bournemouth Belle' and its pristine Pullmans on 9 May 1966. I sometimes wondered if it wouldn't be better practice to have three or four cleaned engines ready for use on such a prestigious train. Entering traffic in October 1945, No. 34012 was rebuilt in January 1958 and withdrawn in December 1966.

At the end if its epic record-breaking run up from Southampton (76 minutes without breaking the line limit of 85 mph), Merchant Navy No. 35008 *Orient Line* looks ready to do it all over again! This photograph was taken on 6 July 1967. The loco entered traffic in June 1942, was rebuilt in May 1957 and was withdrawn in July 1967.

Approaching New Milton with an eastbound Bournemouth to Waterloo service, Nine Elms West Country No. 34031 *Torrington* is looking very smart on 22 April 1962. Introduced to traffic in June 1946, No. 34031 was rebuilt in November 1958 and withdrawn in February 1965.

Producing a healthy plume of 'clag' and in a filthy condition, West Country No. 34034 *Honiton* charges through New Milton with a Waterloo-bound service on 1 February 1967. *Honiton* entered traffic in July 1946, was rebuilt in August 1960 and was withdrawn at the end of SR steam in July 1967.

With only two months to go before withdrawal, Eastleigh's Battle of Britain No. 34058 *Sir Frederick Pile* hurries past New Milton's goods yard with a westbound Weymouth express on 15 August 1964. This loco was introduced to traffic in April 1947, rebuilt in November 1960 and withdrawn in October 1964.

Nicely clean but sadly without nameplates, Merchant Navy No. 35023 *Holland-Afrika Line* is at speed through New Milton with a Weymouth-bound express on 2 December 1966. Entering traffic in November 1948, No. 35023 was rebuilt in February 1957 and withdrawn at the end of SR steam in July 1967.

The detritus of electrification works lies all around as West Country No. 34040 *Crewkerne* drifts into New Milton with a Bournemouth to Waterloo service on 11 November 1966. She entered traffic in September 1946, was rebuilt in October 1960 and was withdrawn in July 1967.

One of my favourite Merchant Navy shots. With just a couple of miles to go, Bournemouth's No. 35013 *Blue Funnel* erupts through Boscombe with a Waterloo to Weymouth express on 8 April 1965. Entering traffic in February 1945, No. 35013 was rebuilt in May 1956 and withdrawn in July 1967.

In an uncharacteristically grimy condition, Salisbury's West Country No. 34026 *Yes Tor* enters New Milton station with an eastbound service for Waterloo on 26 February 1966. *Yes Tor* entered traffic in April 1946 and was then rebuilt in February 1958. She was withdrawn in September 1966.

Hauling a train of three condemned locomotives, including No. 34045 *Ottery St Mary*, No. 34105 *Swanage* and Q Class No. 30541, Battle of Britain No. 34051 *Winston Churchill* is taking water at Salisbury before heading up the Wylye Valley to Westbury on 22 February 1965. In the opposite platform, in the distance, is No. 34007 *Wadebridge* on a train for Yeovil. Entering traffic in December 1946, No. 34051 was eventually withdrawn in September 1965.

A bit close for comfort, Merchant Navy No. 35030 *Elder-Dempster Lines* hurries through New Milton with the westbound 'Bournemouth Belle' on 12 June 1965. As well as being the last Merchant Navy to be built, No. 35030 also hauled the last SR steam service on 9 July 1967. Entering service in April 1949, No. 35030 was rebuilt in April 1958 and was withdrawn at the end of steam in July 1967.

West Country No. 34015 *Exmouth* rests on Weymouth shed on 30 August 1965. This loco was shedded at either Exmouth Junction or Salisbury throughout its lifetime in traffic. Entering service in November 1945, *Exmouth* was eventually withdrawn in April 1967.

Through the verdant cutting of Hinton Bank, Salisbury's Battle of Britain No. 34056 *Croydon* plunges down the gradient with a Waterloo to Weymouth express on 16 July 1965. Entering traffic in February 1947, No. 34056 was rebuilt in December 1960 and withdrawn in May 1967.

Eastleigh's West Country No. 34041 *Wilton* hurries down Hinton Bank with a westbound inter-regional service from Sheffield on 16 July 1965. *Wilton* was introduce to traffic in October 1946 and was withdrawn in January 1966.

With an old school mate, now a Bournemouth Fireman, waving from the cab, Battle of Britain No. 34052 *Lord Dowding* races along the Christchurch embankment with a Bournemouth to Waterloo service on 13 March 1965. Now a preserved engine, No. 34052 entered traffic in December 1946 and was rebuilt in September 1958. She was withdrawn in July 1967 at the end of SR steam.

Hauling a westbound railtour through New Milton, West Country No. 34021 *Dartmoor* appears to be in fine fettle on 6 May 1967. Five days before the end of SR steam, I had a fine run behind this loco between Southampton and Waterloo, achieving a net time of 76 min. 30 secs over 79.25 miles. The loco was introduced to traffic in January 1946 and was rebuilt in December 1957. She was withdrawn in July 1967.

On a dull day, Merchant Navy No. 35029 *Ellerman Lines* is steam tight and going well through New Milton with a Weymouth to Waterloo express on 20 May 1966. In this image the size of a Merchant Navy boiler shows up well. The loco entered traffic in February 1949 and was rebuilt in September 1959. It was withdrawn in September 1966.

The 'Channel Islands Boat Express' runs fast through New Milton behind Merchant Navy No. 35028 *Clan Line* on 9 June 1967. Note the interesting six-wheeled parcels van behind the tender. *Clan Line* entered traffic in December 1948 and was rebuilt in October 1959. She was withdrawn in July 1967.

Nine Elms West Country No. 34037 *Clovelly* is about to plunge through the Station Road overbridge and New Milton station with a westbound Weymouth express on 19 August 1966. I had an excellent run from Waterloo to Southampton behind No. 34037 in May 1967, logging a net time of 79 min. 15 sec. for the 79.25 miles.

In the 'parkland' setting of Hinton Bank, a beautifully clean Battle of Britain, and Bournemouth 'good 'un,' No. 34085 *501 Squadron* plunges down the grade with a Waterloo to Weymouth service on 25 June 1965. Introduced to traffic in November 1948, No. 34085 was rebuilt in June 1960 and withdrawn in September 1965.

Another Battle of Britain descending Hinton Bank, Bournemouth's No. 34053 *Sir Keith Park* is heading a Saturdays-only inter-regional service from Sheffield to Bournemouth on 25 June 1965. Entering traffic in January 1947, *Sir Keith* was rebuilt in November 1958 and withdrawn in October 1965.

A quiet Sunday morning at New Milton and Merchant Navy No. 35011 *General Steam Navigation* pulls out of the station with a Waterloo to Bournemouth service. Bob the signalman can be seen doing a bit of station portering. The loco entered traffic in December 1944 and was rebuilt in July 1959. She was withdrawn in February 1966.

During a period of single line working between New Milton and Sway, the fireman of Battle of Britain No. 34052 *Lord Dowding* has delivered the tablet to the signalman and now the driver lifts the regulator to draw a westbound service out of the Up platform. *Lord Dowding* entered service in December 1946 and was rebuilt in September 1958. She was withdrawn in July 1967 and passed into preservation.

Driver 'Stooge' Wilmore relaxes for a bit while passengers disembark from a Waterloo to Bournemouth train at New Milton on 25 July 1965. The engine is West Country No. 34019 *Bideford*. Although rather grimy, the loco is steam tight and still has its nameplates. Entering service in December 1945, No. 34019 was eventually withdrawn in March 1967.

During the beautiful summer of 1964, Salisbury's West Country No. 34032 *Camelford* drifts down Hinton Bank with an Eastleigh to Bournemouth local on 5 August. *Camelford* was introduced to traffic in June 1946, rebuilt in October 1960 and withdrawn in October 1966.

With the words 'Steam for Ever' chalked on its smokebox door, West Country No. 34009 *Lyme Regis* stands proud on Bournemouth Shed on 12 September 1964. The loco was transferred from Nine Elms to Eastleigh just two days later. Entering traffic in September 1945, No. 34009 was rebuilt in June 1960 and withdrawn in June 1967.

Nine Elms' cleaners have done a superb job on Merchant Navy No. 35017 *Belgian Marine*. The engine looks immaculate as it charges up Hinton Bank with a Weymouth to Waterloo express on 6 August 1964. Introduced to traffic in April 1945, No. 35017 was rebuilt in March 1957 and withdrawn in July 1966.

Another immaculate Merchant Navy, Weymouth's No. 35012 *United States Lines* flies past Walkford with a Waterloo to Weymouth express on 9 May 1966. Entering traffic in January 1945, No. 35012 was rebuilt in February 1957 and withdrawn in April 1967.

With just ten days to go before the end of SR steam, West Country No. 34024 *Tamar Valley* has obviously seen railtour duty as it draws out of Bournemouth Central with a Weymouth to Waterloo express on 29 June 1967. The engine entered traffic in February 1946, was rebuilt in February 1961 and withdrawn in July 1967.

An unusual sight on the Bournemouth line, Exmouth Junction's West Country No. 34030 *Watersmeet* passes near Walkford on a Bournemouth to Waterloo train on 7 March 1964. I had previously only ever seen this loco after an overhaul, shunting in New Milton's goods yard in 1962. *Watersmeet* was introduced to traffic in May 1946 and was eventually withdrawn in September 1964.

In the early sixties my older brother John and my friend Eric would usually meet up in our station yard before Sunday lunch to see the Brighton to Bournemouth excursion go through, and then wait a further twenty minutes to see the 10.30 ex-Waterloo. Here, Merchant Navy No. 35012 *United States Lines* is charging through New Milton on a Sunday in November 1962. Entering service in January 1945, No. 35012 was rebuilt in February 1957 and withdrawn in April 1967.

In the days of steam, banks of wild flowers thrived in the environment of summer fires and steam vapour. Here, Battle of Britain No. 34052 *Lord Dowding* hurries westward with a Waterloo to Weymouth express between New Milton and Hinton on 13 June 1965. *Lord Dowding* entered traffic in December 1946 and was rebuilt in September 1958. She was withdrawn in July 1967.

The original Bulleid Pacific rebuild, Nine Elms Merchant Navy No. 35018 *British India Line* brakes for the Lymington Junction speed restriction while heading a Weymouth to Waterloo express on 3 May 1962. Entering traffic in May 1945, No. 35018 was rebuilt in February 1956 and withdrawn in August 1964.

Looking smart on Bournemouth Shed, Eastleigh's Battle of Britain No. 34079 *141 Squadron* awaits its next duty on 28 February 1965. The loco was introduced to traffic in July 1948 and was withdrawn in February 1966.

Glinting in the winter sunshine, Nine Elms West Country No. 34006 *Bude* is steam tight and going well as she powers up Hinton Bank with a two-hour Bournemouth to Waterloo express on 15 November 1961. The first Bulleid Pacific I ever saw, *Bude* was introduced to traffic in August 1945 and withdrawn in March 1967.

Taken from a Reading-bound DMU on 28 July 1964, Nine Elms Merchant Navy No. 35024 *East Asiatic Company* hurries westward at Worting Junction with a Waterloo to Weymouth express. This loco entered traffic November 1948 and was rebuilt in April 1949. She was withdrawn in January 1965.

Obviously recently overhauled and looking superb in the morning sun, Nine Elms Merchant Navy No. 35029 *Ellerman Lines* awaits its next duty on Bournemouth Shed on 25 June 1963. *Ellerman Lines* entered traffic in February 1949 and was rebuilt in September 1959. She was withdrawn in September 1966.

Exmouth Junction's Battle of Britain No. 34076 *41 Squadron* is a rare visitor to the Bournemouth line on 14 June 1964. She is heading an inter-regional service from Bournemouth to York. Entering service in June 1948, the loco was withdrawn in January 1966.

Another balmy day at New Milton and Eastleigh's Battle of Britain No. 34060 *35 Squadron* passes through with a Sheffield to Bournemouth inter-regional service on 30 July 1965. She was introduced to traffic in April 1947 and rebuilt in November 1960. The loco was withdrawn at the end of SR steam in July 1967.

Entering New Milton with an Eastleigh to Bournemouth local on 16 July 1965, Eastleigh's West Country No. 34023 *Blackmore Vale* was eventually purchased for preservation and stored at the Longmoor Military Railway before removal to the Bluebell Line. The loco entered traffic in February 1946 and was withdrawn in July 1967.

Captured on 20 April 1967, Merchant Navy No. 35007 *Aberdeen Commonwealth* is highlighted by the setting sun as she dashes through New Milton with a Waterloo to Weymouth express. Pigeon fanciers to the right hardly take any notice! The loco entered traffic in June 1942 and was rebuilt in May 1958. She was withdrawn at the end of SR steam in July 1967.

West Country No. 34021 *Dartmoor* hurries past Milepost 98.75 with a Waterloo to Weymouth express on 12 May 1967. I had several excellent runs behind this loco in the last year of SR steam. *Dartmoor* was introduced in January 1946, rebuilt in December 1957 and withdrawn in July 1967.

Eastleigh Battle of Britain No. 34088 *213 Squadron* creates some drama in the setting sun as she powers through New Milton with a Weymouth to Waterloo express on 30 January 1967. Entering traffic in December 1948, No. 34088 was rebuilt in April 1960 and withdrawn in March 1967.

It's a chilly dusk and Merchant Navy No. 35013 *Blue Funnel* flies eastward at Ashley with a two-hour Bournemouth to Waterloo express on 6 January 1963. *Blue Funnel* entered traffic in February 1945. She was rebuilt in May 1956 and withdrawn in July 1967.

West Country No. 34037 *Clovelly* pulls out of New Milton with a Waterloo to Bournemouth service on 28 October 1966. Driven by Nine Elms Driver F. H. Walker, I had a superb run from Waterloo to Southampton behind No. 34037 in May 1967. *Clovelly* entered traffic in August 1946 and was rebuilt in March 1958. She was withdrawn in July 1967.

Simmering at Waterloo after a non-stop run from Bournemouth, Merchant Navy No. 35030 *Elder-Dempster Lines* is suffering from a hot box after an attempt to achieve a record time for the run. She entered traffic in April 1949 and was rebuilt in April 1958. She was withdrawn in July 1967.

On a bright winter's morning, Bournemouth Merchant Navy No. 35021 *New Zealand Line* has a heavy train as it heads east along the Christchurch embankment with a Weymouth to Waterloo express on 15 November 1961. This loco entered traffic in September 1948 and was rebuilt in June 1959. She was withdrawn in August 1965.

Nine Elms Fireman Len Butler is in the driver's seat of West Country No. 34023 *Blackmore Vale* as she gets underway at New Milton with a Waterloo to Bournemouth service on 29 October 1966. The loco entered traffic in February 1946 and was withdrawn in July 1967.

Weymouth's Merchant Navy No. 35012 *United States Lines* looks in good nick as she restarts a service for Waterloo away from Pokesdown on 9 March 1965. Entering traffic in January 1945, No. 35012 was rebuilt in February 1957 and withdrawn in April 1967.

Making good progress along the Christchurch embankment, West Country No. 34044 *Woolacombe* is at the head of a Weymouth to Waterloo express on 16 January 1965. *Woolacombe* entered traffic in October 1946 and was rebuilt in May 1960. She was withdrawn in May 1967.

Salisbury's beautifully clean West Country No. 34108 *Wincanton* pauses at New Milton with a westbound Waterloo to Bournemouth service on 28 May 1966. This loco entered service in April 1950 and was rebuilt in April 1961. She was withdrawn in June 1967.

A wintery scene on 7 November 1962 and Bournemouth's West Country No. 34029 *Lundy* heads east with a two-hour Bournemouth to Waterloo express. *Lundy* entered traffic in May 1946 and was rebuilt in December 1958. She was withdrawn in September 1964.

The 'Channel Islands Boat Express' hurries up through New Milton behind Weymouth's Merchant Navy No. 35012 *United States Lines* on 2 September 1966. This loco entered traffic in January 1945 and was rebuilt in February 1957. It was withdrawn in April 1967.

Appearing to have a leaking gland, Nine Elms West Country No. 34002 *Salisbury* is about to plunge through New Milton's Station Road bridge with a Waterloo to Weymouth express on 4 September 1965. *Salisbury* entered traffic in June 1945 and was eventually withdrawn in April 1967.

Heading the 'Channel Islands Boat Express', Eastleigh's West Country No. 34018 *Axminster* hurries east near Stem Lane on 20 May 1966. This loco entered traffic in December 1945 and was rebuilt in September 1958. She was withdrawn in July 1967.

Nicely clean, Nine Elms West Country No. 34009 *Lyme Regis* waits at New Milton with a Down Waterloo to Bournemouth service on 14 June 1964. Entering service in September 1945, No. 34009 was rebuilt in January 1961 and withdrawn in October 1966.

Erupting out of the setting sun, No. 34008 *Padstow* is steam tight and going well with a Waterloo-bound express through New Milton on a wintry 27 December 1964. *Padstow* entered traffic in September 1945 and was rebuilt in June 1960. She was withdrawn in June 1967.

A sylvan scene on Hinton Bank and Salisbury's immaculate Battle of Britain No. 34051 *Winston Churchill* passes with a westbound express for Weymouth on 25 September 1964. The loco was introduced to traffic in December 1946 and withdrawn in September 1965.

Nine Elms West Country No. 34038 *Lynton* is going well near Walkford with a westbound service for Bournemouth on 29 May 1966. *Lynton* entered traffic in September 1946 and was withdrawn in June 1966.

Bournemouth Fireman Ronald Whittaker chats to the driver of Battle of Britain No. 34087 *145 Squadron* as he prepares to pull out of Bournemouth with the 'Bournemouth Belle' on 23 May 1965. Entering traffic in December 1948, No. 34087 was rebuilt in December 1960 and withdrawn in July 1967.

Hauling a short parcels train through New Milton, Merchant Navy No. 35027 *Port Line* should be powering more substantial traffic on 1 May 1966. *Port Line* entered traffic in December 1948 and was rebuilt in May 1957. She was withdrawn in September 1966.

On 18 April 1967, westbound West Country No. 34095 *Brentor* accelerates away from single line working at New Milton while another West Country comes forward to enter the section. *Brentor* entered traffic in October 1949 and was rebuilt in January 1961. It was withdrawn in July 1967.

A morning service for Waterloo accelerates away from a stop at New Milton headed by West Country No. 34024 *Tamar Valley* on 30 January 1967. Entering traffic in February 1946, No. 34024 was rebuilt in February 1961 and withdrawn in July 1967.

On a hot summer's afternoon in 1964, Salisbury's Battle of Britain No. 34059 *Sir Archibald Sinclair* has just passed through Hinton Admiral with a Weymouth to Waterloo express on 7 July 1964. Entering traffic in April 1947, No. 34059 was rebuilt in March 1960 and withdrawn in May 1966.

New Milton's goods yard as it was, while in the background Merchant Navy No. 35008 *Orient Line* speeds east with a Weymouth to Waterloo express on 9 May 1966. Introduced into traffic in June 1942, No. 35008 was rebuilt in May 1957 and withdrawn at the end of SR steam in July 1967.

Driver John Noel and Fireman Dave Tomlin bask in the sun on board West Country No. 34025 *Whimple* at New Milton while waiting for the 'right away' with an Eastleigh to Bournemouth local on 1 July 1967. *Whimple* entered traffic in March 1946 and was rebuilt in October 1957. She was withdrawn in July 1967.

West Country No. 34104 *Bere Alston* draws into New Milton with a Waterloo-bound service on 3 March 1967. I travelled behind this loco quite often on my weekly commutes to Waterloo from the New Forest. *Bere Alston* was introduced to traffic in April 1950, rebuilt in May 1961 and withdrawn in June 1967. It was the last Bulleid Pacific to be rebuilt.

West Country No. 34102 *Lapford* gets on the move at New Milton with a Bournemouth to Waterloo service on 3 March 1967. Entering service in March 1950, No. 34102 was withdrawn in July 1967. *Lapford* was the last original Bulleid Pacific to run in BR service.